Disorderly Conduct

W·W·NORTON & COMPANY·NEW YORK·LONDON

Disorderly Conduct

VERBATIM EXCERPTS
FROM ACTUAL CASES

RODNEY R. JONES
CHARLES M. SEVILLA
GERALD F. UELMEN

The text of this book is composed in Avanta, with display type set in Mistral and
Helvetica Bold. Composition and manufacturing by The Haddon Craftsmen, Inc.
Book design by Debra Morton Hoyt

First Edition

Library of Congress Cataloging-in-Publication Data

Jones, Rodney R.
  Disorderly conduct.

  1. Trials—United States—Anecdotes, facetiae,
satire, etc. I. Sevilla, Charles M. II. Uelmen,
Gerald F. III. Title.
K184.J66   1987   347.73'7   87–5660

ISBN 0-393-02456-3   347.3077

W. W. Norton & Company, Inc., 500 Fifth Avenue, New York, N. Y. 10110
W. W. Norton & Company Ltd., 37 Great Russell Street, London WC1B 3NU

1 2 3 4 5 6 7 8 9 0

To the lawyers who work in the pits,
and manage to keep their sense of humor.

CONTENTS

Foreword   9

 1   Judicial Temperament   13
 2   The Pleadings   29
 3   Police Investigation   39
 4   Accident Reports   49
 5   The Advocates   57
 6   Picking a Jury   65
 7   The Defendant   75
 8   Witnesses   85
 9   Leading Questions   97
10   Cross Examination   109
11   Expert Witnesses   119
12   Creative Defenses   131
13   Closing Arguments   141
14   Jury Instructions and Deliberations   151
15   Sentencing   161

FOREWORD

Each of the vignettes appearing in this book actually took place in a courtroom. While the vast majority occurred in courtrooms of the United States, we have occasionally reached across the border to Canada, or even across the ocean to England. While the drama which takes place in courtrooms is frequently portrayed by the media, the humor is too often overlooked. It is all preserved, however, in the verbatim transcripts taken down by Court Reporter. Those were our primary source.

Many of the selections have appeared in a bimonthly column by Charles M. Sevilla, called "Great Moments in Courtroom History," published in both the *Forum* of California Attorneys for Criminal Justice and the *Champion* of the National Association of Criminal Defense Lawyers. We have also drawn on the collection of Judge William B. Burleigh of the Monterey, California Municipal Court, and the occasional excerpts published in *Dicta*, the magazine of the San Diego Bar Association. Permission is gratefully acknowledged.

Rodney R. Jones
Charles M. Sevilla
Gerald F. Uelmen

Disorderly Conduct

1

JUDICIAL
TEMPERAMENT

"The acme of judicial distinction means the ability to look a lawyer straight in the eyes for two hours and not hear a damn word he says."
CHIEF JUSTICE JOHN MARSHALL

"Impartial, adj: Unable to perceive any promise of personal advantage from espousing either side of a controversy or adopting either of two conflicting opinions."
AMBROSE BIERCE

"If I had me a job to pick out, I'd be a judge. I've looked over all th' others and that's th' on'y wan that suits. I have th' judicyal timperamint. I hate wurruk."
MR. DOOLEY (FINLEY PETER DUNNE)

THE COURT	I am very careful in these cases.
COUNSEL	I understand.
THE COURT	I am more careful in these cases than any other. The jury gets the case purely from the evidence. I can be so impeccably fair.
COUNSEL	I never questioned your fairness. I beg the indulgence of the court.
THE COURT	This is something you have to be born with, a gift.
COUNSEL	I concede this.
THE COURT	I have that gift. It is a tremendous gift and not many judges have the tremendous gift of fairness. It is something that I have to admit, and I admit it with a great deal of pride, but with a great deal of humility. I have it. I have an information, so to speak. It is what has made me a good student in constitutional law. I suppose so. It is what made it possible for me to perhaps pass the bar examination without an error in the entire examination that I went through.

I have that gift of fairness. I also have a gift of comprehensive thinking. I think all the way around every subject and get its interrelated parts and put them together as I go piece by piece, step by step. I have this, and I almost have the gift of reading minds and the thoughts of the individual.

. . . .

THE COURT	A curse on you, Kittle [the prosecutor] and a curse on your house and the whole damned Federal Crown for setting these cases down on Friday. I've told you about this before. Get a transcript with my profanity, Kittle, and give it to whoever is in charge there.
PROSECUTOR	Your Honor, this matter was set down by appearance not by—
THE COURT	I know, Kittle. You don't send out the instructions. Just a minute. I'll deal with it right now. Give me the information and if you do that, which I suspect you won't, Kittle, tell them I had a scowl on my face.
PROSECUTOR	Very well, Your Honor.
THE COURT	All right, read the charge.
CLERK	Joseph Arthur M., you are charged that at the City of Vancouver, Province of British Columbia, on the 25th day of January, A.D. 1979 you did unlawfully possess a narcotic, to wit, cannabis (marijuana), contrary to the provisions of the Narcotic Control Act. How do you plead to this charge, guilty or not guilty?
DEFENDANT	Guilty.
THE COURT	Go ahead, Mr. Kittle, tell me the heinous circumstances surrounding this offense.
PROSECUTOR	At approximately 2:15 a.m., January 25, a search was being conducted of the accused's room. He was found lying on the bed awake and in between the mattresses was found one plastic baggie containing

five small plastic baggies containing suspected marijuana. A conversation ensued. "Do you know what this is?" Answer, "Yes." Question, "Is it Michelle's?" Answer, "No." And there was further conversation which I think is unnecessary in this respect.

THE COURT   Any record?

PROSECUTOR   I have none, Your Honor.

THE COURT   How old are you, M?

DEFENDANT   Nineteen.

THE COURT   How long have you lived in Vancouver?

DEFENDANT   Off and on for the last two years.

THE COURT   Are you living with your parents or on your own?

DEFENDANT   On my own.

THE COURT   What do you do for a living?

DEFENDANT   I'm an insulator by trade on an apprenticeship.

THE COURT   You won't know why I'm doing this, M., because I think you're a useless idle bum who pretends to be a citizen of Canada and flagrantly breaks the law of Canada doing little or no good to yourself or your country. I have not much use for you or your type, a bunch of long-haired freaks, and you won't understand why I'm giving you an absolute discharge, but I'm doing it because I'm vexed with the Crown. An absolute discharge. Get out. No one will ever know how lucky you are. You certainly won't. You haven't got the

brains. Tell them that too, would you,
Kittle, and tell them that's the Friday
routine from here on in.

PROSECUTOR Yes, Your Honor.

. . . .

COUNSEL I want the record also to reflect that the
court has made noises on the record
indicating a "tsk" sort of sound, so that
the record can at least show . . .

THE COURT For the record, it is spelled t-s-k, I think.
Well, Counsel, I would like the record to
reflect that your attitude is petulant,
childlike and totally and thoroughly
unprofessional.

COUNSEL I respectfully disagree with the court.

THE COURT Well, you have your right to disagree, but
we have disagreed before and I certainly
disagree with you now. The record is
probably as long as you are tall already
about statements that have been made by
you.

COUNSEL The record should reflect that I'm short,
Your Honor.

THE COURT Well, the record may also reflect that my
patience with you has about reached the
point of your height as well.

. . . .

THE COURT [to defense attorney]: The court suggests
to you that the questioning of this witness

	has been exhausted. You have three more minutes. No more.
COUNSEL	I am sorry, Your Honor. I am sorry I have irritated you.
THE COURT	You are not irritating me at all, sir. You have a perfect right to make a record.
COUNSEL	Your Honor, you yelled—you have yelled at me twice within the last two minutes. You are scowling at me now. You tell me I only have three minutes left and then you tell me I am not irritating you. Your Honor, I am sorry, but I can't help when you yell at me but feel that I have irritated you.
THE COURT	I am not yelling at you at all.
COUNSEL	Not at this moment you are not, Your Honor, but you have yelled at me twice in the last two minutes.
THE COURT	Well, I don't agree with you that I have yelled at you.
COUNSEL	You are pointing your fingers at me, Your Honor.
THE COURT	Just a moment.
COUNSEL	You are pointing your fingers at me, sir.
THE COURT	I am not.
COUNSEL	You are pointing two fingers at me this very minute, Your Honor. Would you please not point at me like that? You are still pointing.
THE COURT	Counsel, Counsel.
COUNSEL	Yes, Your Honor.
THE COURT	Please remember that you are addressing a Superior Court Judge and behave yourself.

19

COUNSEL   I am.

THE COURT   Now, I am making my ruling and I said
            you only have three more minutes. That's
            all you have. Is that clear? Now, if you
            interpret that as shouting you may do so.
            Now please proceed.

COUNSEL   Your Honor, I wonder if we might have a
            recess. Frankly, Your Honor, I am upset.
            May we have a recess for a few minutes?

THE COURT   Well, that's a reasonable request. How
            long a recess do you want?

COUNSEL   Oh, I think ten minutes would be enough.

THE COURT   Sir?

COUNSEL   Ten minutes.

THE COURT   Ten minute recess.

. . . .

COUNSEL   In this case, my defense disputes the
            seriousness of the injury; no medical
            attention, no sutures, no loss of
            consciousness, nothing. In fact, when I last
            saw the young gentleman, the remnant
            was a black eye, which I don't think
            comes under the purview of serious injury.

D.A.   Yeah.

THE COURT   Mr. Prosecutor?

D.A.   Just observing. I wonder how it feels to
            get punched in the mouth. I wonder if
            that's a 242 or 245.

THE COURT   You may find out if you keep on
            interrupting.

20

"I'd give it another five minutes, Your Honor. The tension's beginning to mount."

. . . .

COUNSEL   Judge, may I be heard on the matter of bond on appeal and possible stay of execution of the sentence?

THE COURT   Yes. Denied.

. . . .

D.A.   Is Your Honor saying that the magistrate should have gone into the 100 investigations that the officer talks about at page 413? Is that what you're saying?

THE COURT   I've just read 800 pages of your argument and questions, and let me instruct you, let me direct you that I do not like and will not accept the Socratic form of argument.

D.A.   All right.

THE COURT   Do not ask the Court a question again.

D.A.   All right. Is Your Honor saying . . .

. . . .

THE COURT   The amount of fees being asked for—what does this mean, "Multiplied by three," Mr. W.?

COUNSEL   Your Honor, there is authority for a multiplication factor based upon the difficulty of the case.

THE COURT   Can you tell me what was difficult about this case?

COUNSEL   Well, Your Honor, basically dealing with

Your Honor is what was difficult about the case.

THE COURT What was that again? I didn't hear.

COUNSEL I said dealing with Your Honor was what was difficult.

THE COURT Mr. W., you know I find you particularly offensive and I want you to know.

COUNSEL Your Honor—

THE COURT Now just a minute. Don't you come in to this courtroom and make a remark like that.

COUNSEL Your Honor asked me the question.

THE COURT I have stood you enough in this courtroom. This petition is denied. The Government doesn't have to answer it.

COUNSEL Very well, Your Honor. I also ask you to expunge some remarks that you made gratuitously in an order.

THE COURT That motion is denied.

COUNSEL And Your Honor continues to make gratuitous remarks and continues to—

THE COURT That motion is denied.

COUNSEL Thank you very much, Your Honor.

. . . .

THE COURT Sir, I have no intention of waiting for courts of appeal. They are no longer courts. They are nothing except snags for time. Period.

COUNSEL Well, I'm not indicating that we should.

THE COURT I have long since given up; long, long

since given up. As far as I'm concerned the appellate situation in this state is a horror. It makes the trial situation equally poor. And if we sit around waiting for those people to take a laxative, it's the slowest working laxative in the world. I have been given a responsibility and by God I'm going to carry it out. And the blessed Supreme Court can sit up there as long as it wants and die of old age. I'm not going to wait on them to say anything anymore. I've waited and waited and waited for twenty years. Forget it.

. . . .

COUNSEL Shot down again.

THE COURT Any other foundations upon which you would like to urge the admissibility of this?

COUNSEL It's going to take your overruling my—

THE COURT That's fine. I am pleased to do it.

COUNSEL I don't want you to be pleased to do it. I would like for you to say it's a very close question.

THE COURT This is an extremely close question. But having delicately balanced the points of law in favor and the points of law opposed, I am obligated, in following the mandates of the Evidence Code and the higher courts, despite any personal feelings I may have to the contrary, because my duty here is not to impose my personal feelings on my rulings, but to follow the law. And this is one of those occasions where I am discharging my duties solely and simply. And I wouldn't admit this Goddamn thing if you paid me.

. . . .

D.A. Did you say that to the investigating officer?

WITNESS Didn't I tell you I couldn't remember back that far?

D.A. So, you don't remember saying that? Is that what you are telling me? You don't remember?

WITNESS I know what I just told you. Do you?

THE COURT Did you say that to the officer?

WITNESS What did I just say?

THE COURT I'm asking you to answer my question.

WITNESS I just told you if I can't remember back that far how in the hell am I going to answer it?

THE COURT Lucky you are inside, I can see that.

WITNESS Yeah, stupid, they made you a judge, didn't they?

THE COURT Yes, that is right, but I am on the outside.

WITNESS That is all right, asshole. I will be out there soon.

. . . .

THE COURT I would like to cite you for contempt of court—don't say anything until I finish—

25

every time you say something I will cite
you for contempt.

I ruled on your motion and then you
pointed a finger at the court in the
immediate view and presence of the court,
and you were waving your arms and
fingering at me and shouting.

Next count, when both counsel were
coming into my chambers yesterday to
discuss the jury instructions you were
laughing and talking loud as you came into
chambers completely ignoring my presence
in my own chambers. For a whole minute
you were not even facing me. You were
talking to Mr. K. and telling him some
story with loud laughter.

Today at 9:15 A.M., your chair was
positioned sideways 40 degrees tilted. You
were facing the jurors, not the court when
I came in.

Next count, you were playing fingers on
the counsel table like playing piano so loud
that it disturbed the court, and I observed
the court reporter looking at your face.

In the morning when I came into the
courtroom at 9:00 I said "Good morning"
to you and to the prosecutor. You, as usual
for the past five days, you didn't even look
at me. You were whistling.

Now, to these counts what do you have
—would you like to explain something
away before I decide what to do with you?

COUNSEL   You catch me completely—

THE COURT   Are you apologizing?

COUNSEL   If you were offended, absolutely. I would apologize.

THE COURT   Okay. Counsel, I have a son who is about your age. You are very intelligent. Your future is so bright. You are a tremendously great lawyer.

I have been in your position as defense lawyer. Until just yesterday I was sitting right there. I love you. You as a great lawyer must change your attitude, my goodness sake, for your own bright future. You are just—you said eight years. It is just a beginning. You have a bright future ahead of you. Don't screw up, please.

Case dismissed.

. . . .

WITNESS   (prison inmate): I'm not bragging or anything, but I want you to know I've got a law degree from LaSalle and I'm just telling you that so you'll know you're not dealing with a dummy.

THE COURT   I'd like you to know I have a law degree from the University of Washington, and you're not dealing with one either.

. . . .

COUNSEL   Your honor . . .

THE COURT   Don't interrupt.

COUNSEL   But, Your Honor . . .

THE COURT   Don't speak until after I arraign your client.

Sir, you are charged in a four-count indictment with the offenses of assault with a deadly weapon, robbery, mayhem, and receiving stolen property. How do you plead?

COUNSEL   My client doesn't understand English.

. . . .

COUNSEL   Your Honor, I don't mean to be facetious. In all seriousness, this is a case that literally cries out for justice.

THE COURT   Counselor, everyone receives justice in this court.

COUNSEL   Yes, Your Honor, but this case cries out for additional justice.

THE COURT   I'm sorry counselor; we're all out of additional justice. We used it up on the morning calendar.

. . . .

THE COURT   Do you know what Carl Sandburg said?

COUNSEL   "The fog comes in under the cat's feet?"

THE COURT   But he said more cogently, "In the hangman's house we stay off some subjects."

COUNSEL   I see.

THE COURT   Yes.

2

THE PLEADINGS

"In law, it is good policy to never plead what you need not, lest you oblige yourself to prove what you can not."

ABRAHAM LINCOLN

"It is a maxim among these lawyers, that whatever hath been done before, may legally be done again: and therefore they take special care to record all the decisions formerly made against common justice, and the general reason of mankind. These, under the name of precedents, they produce as authorities, to justify the most iniquitous opinions; and the judges never fail of directing accordingly."

JONATHAN SWIFT

The penalty the learned Lord Chancellor, Thomas Egerton (1603–1617), imposed on attorney Richard Mylward for drawing a replication containing 120 pages when, in the Chancellor's opinion, 16 would have sufficed:

"It is therefore ordered that the warden of the Fleet shall take the said Richard Mylward . . . into his custody, and shall bring him unto Westminster Hall on Saturday next . . . and there and then shall cut a hole in the myddest of the same engrossed replication . . . and put the said Richard's head through the same hole, and so let the same replication hang about his shoulders with the written side outward; and then, the same so hanging, shall lead the same Richard, bare headed and bare faced, round Westminster Hall, whilst the courts are sitting, and shall shew him at the bar of every of the three courts within the Hall."

. . . .

A Florida State Prison inmate filed a civil rights suit over allegedly unsanitary prison conditions. He sent the local federal court a plastic envelope containing several dead roaches as evidence of roach infestation. Assuming it was an isolated incident, court officials thought little of the gesture.

Several months later, the prisoner filed a motion for summary judgment and included a separate note that stated, "Dear Mr. Clerk: Please Find enclosed, one (1) mouse and mark as Exhibit M . . . and a motion to the honorable judge."

Court employees dutifully removed the dead rodent from its plastic coffin, placed it in a jar of formaldehyde and filed it with the clerk to preserve the chain of evidence.

But things really got out of hand when the prisoner filed a motion for acceptance for further evidence, and included a less carefully preserved mouse. This exhibit was "a little riper" than the previous specimens, according to court staff.

The judge put an end to the affair ordering the prisoner to content himself with sending written descriptions of such physical evidence.

In addition to probably violating U.S. postal regulations, the judge pointed out, any further such evidence would prompt him to dismiss the case.

. . . .

The following answers to interrogatories were filed by the wife in a divorce action:

52. Do you have a proposal to settle this case amicably?

Answer: Yes.

53. Assuming your answer to the preceding interrogatory is in the affirmative, please state such proposal.

Answer: Use a silver bullet or a wooden stake as is appropriate in these cases.

In Juvenile Court a complaint was filed against a mother under the Welfare and Institutions Code for encouraging a minor to live an immortal life.

Criminal Complaint:

For a further and separate cause of complaint being a different offense from but connected in its commission with the charge(s) set forth in the preceding count(s) hereof, complainant further complainsand says: That said defendant(s), on or about the 17th day of November, 1984, at the County of Monterey, State of California, did commit the crime of VIOLATION of MONTEREY COUNTY ORDINANCE SECTION 11.88.020 a MISDEMEANOR, committed as follows, to-wit: That at said time and place the said defendant(s) did willfully and unlawfully shoot and discharge a fireman within a portion of the unincorporated territory of the County of

Monterey where such shooting and discharging is prohibited.

The primary issue presented on this appeal regards the legal adequacy of the indictment under which Henderson has been tried, convicted and sentenced. That indictment, in pertinent part, reads as follows:

> The Grand Jurors for the State of Mississippi, . . . upon their oaths present: That Jacob Henderson . . . on the 15th day of May, A.D., 1982.
>
> The store building there situated, the property of Metro Auto Painting, Inc., . . . in which store building was kept for sale or use valuable things, to-wit: goods, ware and merchandise unlawfully, feloniously and burglariously did break and enter, with intent the goods, wares and merchandise of said Metro Auto Painting then and there being in said store building unlawfully, feloniously and then and there being in said store building burglariously to take, steal and carry away; And . . . the property of the said Metro Auto Painting then and there being in said store building did then and there unlawfully, feloniously and bur-glariously take, steal and carry away the aforesaid property, he, the said Jacob Henderson, having been twice previously convicted of felonies, to-wit: . . .

"Don't drop it, pal. It's a subpoena."

The remainder of the indictment charges Henderson with being a recidivist.

Henderson, no doubt offended, demurred. In support, he presented an expert witness, Ann Dreher, who had been a teacher of English for nine years. Ms. Dreher testified that, when read consistent with accepted rules of English grammar, the indictment did not charge Jacob Henderson with doing anything; rather it charged that goods, ware and merchandise broke and entered the paint store. The trial judge overruled the objection and the motion, but not without reservation. He stated:

> [T]his same objection has been made numerous times. It is one of Mr. Hailey's pets. [B]ut as far as I know no one has elected to appeal and I'm going to follow the decision whether it is grammatically correct or not. I have repeatedly begged for six years or five years for the district attorney not to use this form. It is very poor English. It is impossible English. . . . In addition to being very poor English, it also charges him with the crime of larceny, which is not necessary to include in an indictment for burglary. I never did understand the reason for that. I again ask the district attorney not to use this form. It's archaic. Even Shakespeare could not understand the grammatical construction of this

indictment. But the objection will be overruled.

Answer to complaint for damages against railroad company:

The defendant further specially excepts to said petition where it is alleged that the plaintiff, upon discovering that the wooden stool was wet, raised the same and squatted with his feet poised on the porcelain bowl of the commode, from which roosting position he says his foot slipped causing him to fall to the great detriment of his left testicle, for the reason that it is obvious that the said commode with its full moon contours was rightfully and properly designed for the comfort of sitters only, being equipped with neither spurs, stirrups nor toeholds for boots or shoes: this defendant, therefore, was not legally required to foresee that the plaintiff, traveling on its modern, air-conditioned deluxe passenger train would so persist in his barnyard predilections as to trample upon its elegant toilet fixture in the barbaric style of horse and buggy days.

For further answer, if needed, this defendant enters its general denial and specially pleads that the plaintiff should not be allowed to recover any sum against it for the reason that the plaintiff

is, in truth and in fact, a chronic
squatter, born and bred to the custom of
the corn crib, and, although a com-
paratively young man, is unable to adapt
himself to the cultural refinements of a
New Deal civilization, and should have,
therefore, in the exercise of due care
deferred taking the Crazy Water Crystals
until such time when he could be at
home secure and sure-footed on his own
dung-hill or with his feet planted solidly
on the flat boards of his own old
fashioned two-holer.

3

POLICE
INVESTIGATION

"The criminal is to go free because the constable has blundered."
JUSTICE BENJAMIN N. CARDOZO

"A policeman's lot is not a happy one."
ARTHUR S. GILBERT

Federal Court of Appeals opinion:

The agents involved speak an almost impenetrable jargon. They do not get into their cars; they enter official government vehicles. They do not get out of or leave their cars, they exit them. They do not go somewhere; they proceed. They do not go to a particular place; they proceed to its vicinity. They do not watch or look; they surveille. They never see anything; they observe it. No one tells them anything; they are advised. A person does not tell them his name; he identifies himself. A person does not say something; he indicates. They do not listen to a telephone conversation; they monitor it. People telephoning to each other do not say "hello"; they exchange greetings. An agent does not hand money to an informer to make a buy; he advances previously recorded official government funds. To an agent, a list of serial numbers does not list serial numbers, it depicts Federal Reserve Notes. An agent does not say what an exhibit is; he says that it purports to be. The agents preface answers to simple and direct questions with "to my knowledge." They cannot describe a conversation by saying "he said" and "I said"; they speak in conclusions. Sometimes it takes the combined efforts of counsel and the judge to get them to state who said what.

Under cross examination, they seem unable to give a direct answer to a question, they either spout conclusions or do not understand. This often gives the prosecutor, under the guise of an objection, an opportunity to suggest an answer, which is then obligingly given.

Police report in a rape case: "The defendant, when first observed, was atop the victim in a sublime position."

. . . .

COUNSEL   Would you observe these photographs and tell me if these items were seen by you that day?

POLICE OFFICER   Yes, sir, all items depicted in the five photos were later observed by this officer while I was observing the said property which was observed in the trunk of the vehicle.

. . . .

Police report description of arrest:
    Defendant was confronted and he again failed to stop and when the officer attempted to stop him by the use of a baton around his neck, defendant freed himself and began moving toward the officer in a threatening manner. The officer struck defendant on the head with

his baton. It was then observed that
defendant appeared to be glassy eyed and
had a distant stare commonly associated
with people under the influence of PCP.

. . . .

COUNSEL	And then after you saw Mr. G, you came up to him—identified yourself?
POLICE OFFICER	Yes, sir.
COUNSEL	Told him in English, probably then in Spanish, that he was under arrest?
POLICE OFFICER	Yes, sir.
COUNSEL	Did you have your weapon drawn as you approached him, sir?
POLICE OFFICER	Indeed I did, sir.
COUNSEL	You told him at this time he was under arrest?
POLICE OFFICER	Yes, sir, I did.
COUNSEL	Mr. G, by the way, was complying with your orders?
POLICE OFFICER	Indeed he was.
COUNSEL	Made no resistance?
POLICE OFFICER	No, sir, he did not.
COUNSEL	Cooperated with you in every way?
POLICE OFFICER	Very cooperative.
COUNSEL	And you had your gun out during this entire period?
POLICE OFFICER	That is correct, sir.
COUNSEL	Where was the gun pointed, sir—at his stomach, midsection, head?
POLICE OFFICER	It was nestled right down the back of his neck.

COUNSEL   Did you say anything to Mr. G, by the way, sir, concerning what would happen if he tried to move or get away?

POLICE OFFICER   I said I would try to blow his head off.

COUNSEL   It was during this time, when Mr. G had that .38 special cradled on the back of his neck, that you told him his rights under Miranda. Is that correct?

POLICE OFFICER   Yes, sir.

. . . .

COUNSEL   Can you tell us what you did with regard to the pat search of Mr. L?

POLICE OFFICER   I began a grasping search of the clothing. And I searched him from the top down until I got to his pants in the groin area and then I felt a hard object.

COUNSEL   And what occurred when you felt that hard object?

POLICE OFFICER   I grabbed at it. I felt the hard object. I grabbed it a little bit closer to try to get the outline of what it was, when L said, "It's my dick."

COUNSEL   And then what happened?

POLICE OFFICER   He said, "I'll get it."

COUNSEL   Officer, you were frightened by what occurred out there; is that right?

POLICE OFFICER   Yes.

COUNSEL   Well what, if anything, had Mr. L done to you that caused you to be frightened? Did telling you you were feeling his dick, did that frighten you?

"I must warn you that anything you say may be taken down and used against you."

POLICE OFFICER   No.

COUNSEL   Did he do anything at all that caused you to be frightened by anything he did or said?

POLICE OFFICER   It became a concern to me when I felt the hard object in his pants, first of all. Then when I continued to feel it and he said, "It's my dick," I got a little more concerned, you know, when he reached in his pants to get that hard object, which I had almost positively identified as a gun.

. . . .

COUNSEL   Where was she?

POLICE OFFICER   In the living room.

COUNSEL   Is that where you placed her under arrest also?

POLICE OFFICER   Yes.

COUNSEL   Did you then unarrest the defendant?

POLICE OFFICER   Yes.

COUNSEL   How did you communicate that to her?

POLICE OFFICER   I told her she wasn't under arrest no more.

COUNSEL   And then did you arrest her again?

POLICE OFFICER   Yes.

COUNSEL   And then did you unarrest her again?

POLICE OFFICER   Yes.

COUNSEL   When did the second unarrest take place?

POLICE OFFICER   When the captain told me I was going to be reprimanded.

COUNSEL   For arresting her or unarresting her?

POLICE OFFICER   No, arresting her.

COUNSEL   So you arrested the lady, the captain told
you to unarrest her, and the captain told
you you would be reprimanded for
arresting her, then you arrested her again?

POLICE OFFICER   I arrested her, the captain told me to
unarrest her, and knowing that the captain
was wrong I arrested her again and then
he told me, well you'd better unarrest her.
And I unarrested her.

. . . .

D.A.   Then what did you do?

POLICE OFFICER   I began kicking in the door.

D.A.   Were you wearing boots?

POLICE OFFICER   Yes, sir, size 12.

D.A.   How many times did you kick the door?

POLICE OFFICER   About ten.

D.A.   What was Sergeant Harp doing while you
were kicking the door?

POLICE OFFICER   Laughing at me.

. . . .

Two police officers extracted a
confession from a suspect by advising him
the Xerox machine was a lie detector.
First they put a colander—a salad strainer
—over the suspect's head and wired it to
the duplicating machine. Then, under the
Xerox lid they placed a slip of paper
reading "He Is Lying!" Every time the

suspect answered a question, an officer would press the duplicating button and out would pop a Xeroxed "He Is Lying!" Finally shaken, the suspect told all. His confession was thrown out by a judge who was not amused.

4

ACCIDENT REPORTS

"It shall be a vexation only to understand the report."
                                              ISAIAH, 28:19

"The reports of my death are greatly exaggerated."
                                              MARK TWAIN

Coming home, I drove into the wrong house and collided with a tree I don't have.

. . . .

The other car collided with mine without giving warning of its intentions.

. . . .

I thought my window was down, but found it was up when I put my hand through it.

. . . .

I collided with a stationary truck coming the other way.

. . . .

A truck backed through my windshield into my wife's face.

. . . .

A pedestrian hit me and went under my car.

. . . .

The guy was all over the road. I had to swerve a number of times before I hit him.

. . . .

I pulled away from the side of the
road, glanced at my mother-in-law, and
headed over the embankment.

. . . .

In my attempt to kill a fly, I drove
into a telephone pole.

. . . .

I had been shopping for plants all day,
and was on my way home. As I reached
an intersection, a hedge sprang up
obscuring my vision. I did not see the
other car.

. . . .

I had been driving my car for forty
years when I fell asleep at the wheel and
had an accident.

. . . .

I was on my way to the doctor's with
rear end trouble when my universal
joint gave way causing me to have an
accident.

. . . .

As I approached the intersection, a stop sign appeared in a place where no stop sign had ever appeared before. I was unable to stop in time to avoid the accident.

. . . .

To avoid hitting the bumper of the car in front, I struck the pedestrian.

. . . .

My car was legally parked as it backed into the other vehicle.

. . . .

An invisible car came out of nowhere, struck my vehicle and vanished.

. . . .

I told the police that I was not injured but on removing my hat, I found that I had a skull fracture.

. . . .

I was sure the old fellow would never make it to the other side of the roadway when I struck him.

. . . .

The pedestrian had no idea which direction to go, so I ran over him.

. . . .

I saw the slow moving, sad-faced gentleman as he bounced off my car.

. . . .

The indirect cause of this accident was a little guy in a small car with a big mouth.

. . . .

I was thrown from my car as it left the road. I was later found in a ditch by some stray cows.

. . . .

The telephone pole was approaching fast. I was attempting to swerve out of its path when it struck my front end.

. . . .

I was unable to stop in time, and my car crashed into the other vehicle. The driver and passengers then left immediately for a vacation with injuries.

. . . .

I was struck by a beer bottle in the
rear head.

. . . .

After approximately two or three
seconds I felt a numbness which came to
my right rear buttock.

5

THE ADVOCATES

"The trial lawyer does what Socrates was executed for: making the worse argument appear the stronger."

JUDGE IRVING KAUFMAN

"Then, if at any time you find you have the worst end of the staff, leave off your cause and fall upon the person of your adversary."

JOHN WILSON

"It isn't the bad lawyers who are screwing up the justice system in this country—it's the good lawyers. If you have two competent lawyers on opposite sides, a trial that should take three days could easily last six months."

ART BUCHWALD

D.A.   Your Honor, prior to calling my first witness, I'd like to state for the record that immediately prior to starting this proceeding and in open court while His Honor was in chambers, defense counsel called me a punk three times and called me a shit once. I don't know what explanation he has for that, but I wanted to put it on the record before we started this. It had to do with this proceeding.

. . . .

D.A.   This matter is here for trial today.
THE COURT   People ready?
D.A.   Yes, but we move to dismiss in the interest of justice.
THE COURT   What is the interest of justice?
D.A.   The case sucks.

. . . .

COUNSEL   That's bullshit. We spent 45 minutes.
THE COURT   You mustn't use bad language because the appellate court doesn't like that. You can say it's nonsense.
COUNSEL   It's nonsense, Your Honor.
THE COURT   That is not a legal objection.

. . . .

COUNSEL   My sole purpose in this little monologue is to record that understanding on the record, and if there is any disagreement with my understanding by counsel for the defendants, which I believe there is not, to ask that that be recorded so that there be no misunderstanding subsequently by any party to this case or any third parties as to what we intend to provide.

THE COURT My problem with what you have said is simply that I am not altogether sure that I understand what you have said.

. . . .

DEFENSE ATTORNEY Then I object to the District Attorney objecting to my objecting to standard legal objections.

. . . .

COUNSEL The D.A. stated that he invited me to discuss these matters with him but so far he has demurred. I think the record should reflect he challenged me to a fight this morning out in the hallway, to go outside and man to man, one to one. I think that's all I need to say.

D.A. Counsel flatters himself. Even in my most frivolous moments I would not consider challenging him to any sort of a fight. I would challenge him to something in the nature of a debate where he might have to look me in the eye and say some of these things that he has said on this document which he snuck under the door this morning. Beyond that, he's a pantywaist.

. . . .

DEFENDANT Judge, I want you to appoint me another lawyer.
THE COURT And why is that?
DEFENDANT Because the P.D. isn't interested in my case.
THE COURT (to public defender) Do you have any comments on defendant's motion?
PUBLIC DEFENDER I'm sorry, Your Honor, I wasn't listening.

. . . .

COUNSEL Your Honor, I have just three or four questions.
THE COURT Oh, come on, Counsel. How can you possibly think of another question?
COUNSEL Well, I had a few minutes, and I was able to.
THE COURT That's enough.
COUNSEL Your Honor, for the record, I do believe I have a right to recross after co-counsel has crossed. It's only three or four questions.
THE COURT I don't give a damn if you have a right. The question is, do you have the sense not to?
COUNSEL Obviously not. I made the request.
THE COURT Ask your question.

61

"If it please the Court, may I point out that I requested
to approach the Bench before learned counsel requested
to approach the Bench."

. . . .

The defendant was charged with murder. After arraignment, the matter of setting bail became a heated issue. The People urged that $50,000 should be the minimum amount because the defendant had a long record.

The deputy public defender was momentarily stunned at the large bail demand, but he regained his composure and said, "That amount of bail is outrageously excessive . . . er well, after all, this is only the defendant's first murder."

. . . .

"Today we conclude that when an attorney for a criminal defendant sleeps through a substantial portion of the trial, such conduct is inherently prejudicial and thus no separate showing of prejudice is necessary. Prejudice is inherent in this case because unconscious or sleeping counsel is equivalent to no counsel at all."

6

PICKING A JURY

"A jury consists of twelve persons of average ignorance."
MARK TWAIN

"The man who wants a jury has a bad case."
JUSTICE OLIVER WENDELL HOLMES, JR.

"A jury consists of 12 persons chosen to decide who has the better lawyer."

ROBERT FROST

THE COURT   Do any of you prospective jurors know
             me?
JUROR   Yes.
THE COURT   I am pleased to see that I have—is our
             acquaintanceship close enough that you
             feel that it might be some impediment
             sitting as a juror?
JUROR   Yes, I feel it would. It's unfavorable.
THE COURT   It is unfavorable? Let's go to some of the
             other questions. You have never had any
             negative experience with law enforcement
             except perhaps sitting as a juror in my
             department; is that correct?
JUROR   No, it wasn't as a juror.
THE COURT   It was not?
JUROR   No.
THE COURT   Was it as a witness?
JUROR   You were the judge in a case that my
             husband was—you denied him a hearing
             for reinstatement to a job with the county.
THE COURT   I see.
JUROR   Twice, in fact.
THE COURT   You didn't testify in the matter?
JUROR   No, I did not.
THE COURT   So that your displeasure with me is merely
             the result of what I did in the case in
             which your husband was involved?
JUROR   Right.
THE COURT   All right. The loser is always displeased, I
             find.
JUROR   I have to live with the loser, though.
THE COURT   Touché. Well, I hope this experience will

be more pleasant for you if you are selected to serve as a juror.

JUROR   We don't think very highly of lawyers either, as a matter of fact.

THE COURT   Okay. When you heard about this case, did you form any opinion about the defendant's guilt or innocence?

JUROR   Not really. I just assumed that he had committed the crime.

. . . .

COUNSEL   Have any of the prospective jurors ever been victims of a crime?

JUROR   Well, I'm not sure if this is considered a victim, but a couple weeks—no, a couple of months ago I was mowing my lawn and there was a guy on my lawn in the nude. That's about the only thing.

COUNSEL   Did you report that to the police?

JUROR   Yes.

COUNSEL   Did they come on to your place then?

JUROR   Yes, right away. It was three officers that came over.

COUNSEL   Did they catch the guy?

JUROR   I don't know. I don't think so.

COUNSEL   Did you give them a description, et cetera, telling the officers what he was doing?

JUROR   Well, I told them what I had seen, but he was a real tall person, so I just saw from the waist down.

. . . .

COUNSEL   Can you participate in an endeavor in
          which the ultimate result might be death
          by lethal injection?

JUROR   They do that up in Huntsville, don't they?
          Yeah, I guess I could do it if it was on a
          weekend.

COUNSEL   And [next juror] you, sir?

JUROR   Yes, I think it's too quick.

COUNSEL   And you, sir?

JUROR   It should be left up to the victims' families
          rather than the courts.

COUNSEL   You know that my client is charged with
          robbing a Seven-Eleven, tying up two
          employees and shooting them both in the
          head as he fled. Now if the state offers
          you evidence to prove these facts, would
          you—

JUROR   He's gone!

. . . .

THE COURT   Were you ever in the service?

JUROR   Yes, the Navy.

THE COURT   How long?

JUROR   29 days.

THE COURT   Without going into detail, why were you
            discharged?

JUROR   They found out I was allergic to wool and
            salt water.

. . . .

THE COURT You feel one side or the other is not starting even here?

JUROR Yes, sir.

THE COURT Is there some particular question that you heard that triggered that?

JUROR No, sir. May I be candid with you?

THE COURT Yes.

JUROR Okay. My daughter is Susan, who was just excused by the D.A.

THE COURT I understand.

JUROR And without being held liable, my personal feelings, I feel the D.A. is a jerk.

THE COURT I think I know enough, Mr. G. It is not necessary to state anything more. You may be excused.

. . . .

Voir dire in a drunk driving case:

COUNSEL Do you think that before the People can prove their case to you, or to all of you beyond a reasonable doubt, that that proof must include scientific evidence that the defendant had blood in his alcohol?

. . . .

COUNSEL Ladies of the jury, the next couple of questions I have to ask you, you may consider them personal in nature. I ask

70

"Are we to understand, then, that you would have no
scruples about imposing the death penalty?"

you please do not consider me to be invading your privacy in any way. Do the concepts of rape and/or sodomy leave you with such a bad taste in your mouth?

. . . .

COUNSEL   If the law or the instructions conflict with your beliefs, will you still accept the law without question?

JUROR   Well, that is what I want to make clear. I don't know what those beliefs are; that is what I have tried to understand. And so I'm finding it difficult to answer that question given those terms used.

COUNSEL   Can you tell us that you would follow the court's instructions regardless of what else happened for you during the course of the trial?

JUROR   Cognitively, yes. Rationally, yes. Emotionally, effectively, I don't know. Or perhaps effectively, yes, and rationally, no.

. . . .

COUNSEL   Did you retain an attorney to represent you in those matters?

JUROR   Yes, I did.

COUNSEL   Were you satisfied with the services of the attorney or attorneys you had?

JUROR   No, I was not.

COUNSEL   Would that carry over to me or to any of the other attorneys?

JUROR   Yes, it would.

COUNSEL   Could you tell me briefly how it would carry over?

JUROR   My opinion of attorneys, that they are one step lower than child molesters.

. . . .

COUNSEL   How do you feel about criminal defense attorneys?

JUROR   I think they should all be drowned at birth.

COUNSEL   Well then, you are obviously biased for the prosecution?

JUROR   What makes you think that, I hate prosecutors too.

. . . .

THE COURT   Is there any reason you could not serve as a juror in this case?

JUROR   I don't want to be away from my job that long.

THE COURT   Can't they do without you at work?

JUROR   Yes, but I don't want them to know it.

. . . .

COUNSEL   Is there anything about your physical condition that might make it difficult for you to serve in this case?

JUROR   No.

COUNSEL You don't have doctor appointments today
or the next couple of days?

JUROR No.

COUNSEL Do you have any physical problems with
your pregnancy?

JUROR I'm not pregnant.

7

THE DEFENDANT

"If there is any truth to the old proverb that 'one who is his own lawyer has a fool for a client,' the Court . . . bestows a constitutional right on the one to make a fool of himself."

JUSTICE HARRY BLACKMUN

"Litigant: A person about to give up his skin for the hope of retaining his bones."

AMBROSE BIERCE

"Most lawyers who win a case advise their clients that 'we have won.' And when justice has frowned upon their cause that 'you have lost.'"

LOUIS NIZER

DEFENDANT I feel that I am being handicapped when the original recess was for me to find things throughout the transcript. I am taken back there. I can't even have a pencil. What possible defense can I have to make notes? Am I to carry a thought in my mind?

THE COURT The pencil problem is an awful problem. The sheriff has a rule that no pencils are allowed, and not even felt pens, and so I have got no control over that.

DEFENDANT The District Attorney has a pen and pencil and everything else. This is not equal defense.

THE COURT The sheriffs have that rule, and it is a good rule. I am sure you understand the reason for it. On the one hand, I expect letting you have a pencil and felt tip pen would be no problem. But suppose somebody in here gets it away from you? That could be a very deadly weapon. You see?

DEFENDANT I can understand that point.

THE COURT How about a crayon? Can't you give him a crayon?

BAILIFF I will check, Your Honor.

THE COURT There is no prohibition on crayon, is there? You can sharpen it up a little bit. I can't make an order that you can have a pencil. I think I will make an order that you can have a crayon, and let's see if the sheriff's department gets that okay.

DEFENDANT	Yes, sir.
BAILIFF	I will try to find one, Your Honor.
THE COURT	Well, I have got some around here.

. . . .

Judge to a defendant: You have a right to a trial by jury, but you may waive that right. Which do you wish to do?

The defendant hesitated. His lawyer said firmly, "Waive." The defendant raised his hand and waved at the judge.

. . . .

THE COURT	You have to say, "I want it," and "I'm willing to give up my rights to have it come on earlier."
DEFENDANT	What rights?
THE COURT	It beats the hell out of me, ma'am. It says there in the Constitution.
DEFENDANT	I don't know what you're talking about, so I can't say.
THE COURT	In that event, we will continue right on as it is. Ma'am, I've got news for you. You've got this; now you're going to have to deal with it, and I don't intend to sit here and conduct a kindergarten playground.
DEFENDANT	I don't understand what you're saying: "Am I willing to give up my rights."
THE COURT	I don't give a good Goddamn whether you said it. All I'm saying is you have a right

to have it come on in 30 days. Now, what is it, ma'am? Is it something in the head there that doesn't click? Very good. We'll enter a plea of not guilty with a jury demand on your behalf. When do you want to go to trial, miss? You're a big girl.

DEFENDANT   I know it, Your Honor. I'm not accustomed to this.

THE COURT   I understand that you're not accustomed to it, but you don't also walk in here and just yence me around. I refuse to be so handled. I'm sorry. I do not intend to be so treated. I've got a number of things to do. I've got a number of people to handle. I've now set trial already for you.

DEFENDANT   Set it whenever you have to. If I'm here, I'm here. If I'm not, I'm not.

. . . .

THE COURT   The charge here is theft of frozen chickens. Are you the defendant, sir?

DEFENDANT   No, sir, I'm the guy who stole the chickens.

. . . .

THE COURT   Are you ready to proceed?

DEFENDANT   No, Your Honor, not at this time. Would you place my matter on second call or recall the case after the court takes a recession?

. . . .

COUNSEL   Now, you indicated that you were missing
           several items?
WITNESS   Yes.
COUNSEL   Cassettes?
WITNESS   Right.
COUNSEL   Do you recall the names of any of those
           cassettes?
WITNESS   Yes, but I couldn't name them all.
COUNSEL   What names do you recall?
WITNESS   Okay. *Rolling Stones Live,* it's a double
           album. Eddie Money, I can't think of the
           other ones.
DEFENDANT Pat Travis?
WITNESS   Right. Pat Travis.
COUNSEL   Shut up.
WITNESS   Two Pat Travis.

. . . .

DEFENDANT Can I ask her some questions?
THE COURT Just one moment.
DEFENDANT This bitch don't know me. She don't
           know who I am.
THE COURT Just one minute, sir. Please, when we
           direct our attention to human beings, we
           use different phraseology, okay?
DEFENDANT I don't give a fuck. This is my fucking
           life.
THE COURT You're going to give a fuck in this court,
           you hear me? You bug off.

80

"Most brilliantly argued self-representation I ever heard."

. . . .

DEFENDANT   Yes, Your Honor. I represented myself on a death penalty case in Santa Monica and I had one pro per on some attempted murder case here in L.A. and Norwalk and Long Beach and some armed robberies. I have been pro per for a few years, Your Honor.

THE COURT   What kind of success have you had in acting as your own lawyer?

DEFENDANT   I didn't get the death penalty, Your Honor.

. . . .

DEFENDANT   I would like to also be allowed movement in the courtroom.

THE COURT   You'd like what?

DEFENDANT   Movement in the courtroom without being followed by the Sheriff.

THE COURT   You can't do that.

DEFENDANT   I think it's inhibiting my defense. It's prejudicial to my defense.

THE COURT   It's up to you. You know, the courthouse, when I first practiced law here, had an iron cage for defendants who are incarcerated and they sat in the iron cage in the courtroom. Even though there is no cage, they still sit in what is a dock and obviously they're not allowed to wander around.

DEFENDANT   They used to feed Christians to lions.
That don't make it right.

. . . .

THE COURT   Each of you present as a defendant has
been charged with a public offense, and
this is the time set for your arraignment.
There will be no defecating or urinating
while I am giving the rights.

. . . .

THE COURT   You've been charged with armed robbery.
Do you want the court to appoint a lawyer
to represent you?

DEFENDANT   You don't have to appoint a very good
lawyer, I'm going to plead guilty.

. . . .

The defendant was in custody. At
arraignment he insisted that a mistake had
been made and that he was not the person
the judge thought he was. He refused to
admit he was the person charged, and
then asked what "that person" was
charged with committing.

THE COURT   Well, there are two cases. The first one is
minor—drunk in public—and if you plead
guilty I would give you credit for time
served and that case would be over. The

second case—battery—is more serious and you should have a lawyer.

DEFENDANT O.K., I'll be that guy on the first case.

. . . .

While working his criminal calendar, the judge called the case of *People v. Steven Lewon Crook.* The bailiff opened the door to the holding cell and called "Crook, come forward." Five prisoners walked from the cell into the courtroom!

. . . .

The defendant, charged with arson, missed a court appearance.

THE COURT Where were you?

DEFENDANT In the hospital.

THE COURT Why?

DEFENDANT Smoke inhalation.

. . . .

DEFENSE COUNSEL Are you sure you did not enter the Seven-Eleven on 40th and N.E. Broadway and hold up the cashier on June 17 of this year?

DEFENDANT I'm pretty sure.

8

WITNESSES

"Wherefore seeing we also are compassed about with so great a cloud of witnesses . . . , let us run with patience the race that is set before us."

HEBREWS, 12:1–2

"Then call them to our presence; face to face; and frowning brow to brow, ourselves will hear the accuser and the accused freely speak."

WILLIAM SHAKESPEARE, RICHARD II

"They cudden't get me into coort as a witness; no, sir, not if't was to hang me best friend. 'T is hard enough with newspapers an' cinsus officers an' th' mim'ry iv cab dhrivers to live down ye'er past without bein' foorced to dhrill it in a r-red coat an' with a brass band ahead befure th' eyes iv th' multitood. I did it wanst; I'll do it no more."

MR. DOOLEY (FINLEY PETER DUNNE)

COUNSEL	(examining a witness with eyesight problems) How many fingers am I holding up?
THE COURT	The record will show the attorney is holding up two fingers.

. . . .

COUNSEL	Do you have any sort of medical disability?
WITNESS	Legally blind.
COUNSEL	Does that create substantial problems with your eyesight as far as seeing things?

. . . .

PROSECUTOR	All right. Do you feel that you got a good look at the face of the person who had pointed that gun at your face initially and took you into the laundry room?
WITNESS	Yes, sir, I do.
PROSECUTOR	If I asked you to look around the courtroom now, do you see the person who pointed that gun at you? If you would like to stand up, you may.
WITNESS	Yes, sir.
PROSECUTOR	You do? Could you please indicate for us where he is located and what he is wearing so we all know who you are talking about?
WITNESS	The gentleman seated at the desk over there.
PROSECUTOR	Okay, I have no further questions.
THE COURT	Seated at what desk over there?

WITNESS   The desk against the wall.

DEFENSE COUNSEL   Your Honor, could the record indicate that the witness has identified the bailiff in the courtroom, who is a deputy sheriff?

THE COURT   He said you identified the deputy sheriff.

WITNESS   I did?

THE COURT   Yeah.

PROSECUTOR   Your Honor, I ask that that man be placed under arrest.

WITNESS   Well, I am sorry. I was going by what I thought I remembered.

THE COURT   I have never had that happen before. That is the first.

WITNESS   Oh, my glasses.

THE COURT   Oh. Can you see better without your glasses?

WITNESS   Yes, Your Honor. The color of the gentleman is the same.

． ． ． ． ． ． ． ． ． ． ． ． ． ． ． ．

WITNESS   The person in the middle is not the one that was—he did not have the gun.

THE COURT   All right, ma'am. But that isn't the question. Let's do it this way. Are you sure that the person without the gun isn't the man on the left?

WITNESS   Yes. I'm sure he is not the one that had the gun.

THE COURT   Oh, no, the one without the gun. Are you sure it's not the person on the left?

WITNESS   Yes, I'm sure.

THE COURT   That he's not?

WITNESS   He's not the one without the gun.

THE COURT Are you sure that the one in the middle is
           the one without the gun?

WITNESS   That's right. I'm sure he's not the one
           without the gun.

COUNSEL   Perhaps the Court could just ask if she
           recognizes him.

. . . .

COUNSEL   Calling your attention now to the
           defendant in the blue shirt, seated at the
           end of the counsel table, do you know
           him?

WITNESS   I have never seen the jerk before.

THE COURT All right. Thank you very much, sir. You
           are excused. You may go.

WITNESS   I am excused, Your Honor?

THE COURT You may go.

WITNESS   (to defendant) I better never see your butt
           in my place again ever.

THE COURT All right, sir. That is enough.

WITNESS   Ever.

. . . .

COUNSEL   Did you give a description of the shirt?

WITNESS   Yes, I did.

COUNSEL   What color was the shirt?

WITNESS   It was a plaid shirt, and I told the deputy
           it had red, possibly some green or blue in
           the shirt, but it was plaid.

COUNSEL   How would you describe it? A dress shirt,

sort of like the one we're wearing, you're
wearing, I'm wearing, or something
different?

WITNESS   I'd describe it as the same shirt that
individual [the defendant] is wearing right
over there today.

· · · · · · · · · · · · · · · ·

THE COURT   All right. Miss, after testifying here and
thinking about it, would you take another
look at this man seated here with defense
counsel?

DEFENSE COUNSEL   Does she need to get closer? I don't have
any objection.

WITNESS   No, this is fine.

THE COURT   You can recognize him all right? You can
see him from where you are seated?

WITNESS   Yes.

PROSECUTOR   Do you want my glasses?

WITNESS   Yes, maybe I will—

THE COURT   No. I'd just as soon she don't have any
glasses. Would you like to get about as
close as you were?

WITNESS   Your Honor, he had more facial hair on
him.

THE COURT   Do you think this is the same person or
not?

WITNESS   If he had that white hat on I would be
able to tell more, because I can't tell with
the receding hairline and—it's hard to tell.

THE COURT   Do you think he is? Do you think he
isn't? Do you know?

"I'm sorry, but counsel *must* take the witness."

WITNESS He had the same face features, like I said earlier. The guy, to me, looked like a street guy.

DEFENSE COUNSEL A what?

WITNESS Somebody who looks on, like, "Laverne and Shirley." They got those two guys on "Laverne and Shirley." That guy that night looked a lot like one of them.

THE COURT Squiggy or Lennie?

. . . .

DEFENSE COUNSEL Now, you wear glasses, don't you?

WITNESS No.

DEFENSE COUNSEL You don't wear glasses?

WITNESS No.

DEFENSE COUNSEL You didn't have glasses on at the lineup?

WITNESS Yes, I did. I don't wear them as a necessity to see. I just wear them to distinctify my vision a little bit better.

. . . .

CLERK Please raise your right hand. You do solemnly swear that the testimony you may give in the cause now pending before this court shall be the truth, the whole truth, and nothing but the the truth, so help you God.

WITNESS No. I don't because I don't even know why I'm here, what I'm here for or nothing. Period. I have no idea why I'm here.

THE COURT	You have been brought in as a witness.
WITNESS	Witness for who?
THE COURT	Brought in as a witness by the district attorney's office.
WITNESS	A witness for the district attorney's office? That's a damn lie. By whose orders? I'd like to know what the hell is going on. I have did nothing. I haven't talked to nobody. I don't know anything what's been happening.
THE COURT	There are no charges against you.
WITNESS	I don't care if there is charges against me. I wouldn't be for the district attorney's office if there were charges against me. Period.
THE COURT	You were brought in as a witness.
WITNESS	Why? From who? Who said what? Who did what? Ain't nobody told me nothing about this shit.
THE COURT	You haven't been asked any any questions.
WITNESS	I'm not going to answer any questions.
THE COURT	You haven't been asked any questions.
WITNESS	I'm not going to answer any questions because I don't know a Goddamn thing. I don't even know why I'm here. I sure like an explanation. They take me out of Folsom with a broken leg Saturday. I ain't got it fixed yet or a cast on it. Hell, no. And regardless, I'm going to tell you out front I have been down over fourteen years and I wouldn't testify for my mother if she was on trial for no district attorney.

That's final. Period. Let me out of here. Don't try this shit no more.

THE COURT Are you going to refuse to be sworn as a witness?

WITNESS I'm refusing everything. I don't even know who's on trial here. Me? For what? I ain't did nothing.

THE COURT You're not on trial here. You were brought in—

WITNESS Who's on trial here?

D.A. Your Honor, I wonder perhaps if the witness might have counsel appointed to represent him?

WITNESS Don't give me no counsel. I don't want no counsel.

D.A. To advise him as to the nature of the proceedings and why he's here to testify.

WITNESS I don't give a fuck why I'm here. Period. I wouldn't help your office. You just go ahead and kill me, brother, because I don't care. I have been a victim for fourteen years. Don't pull this shit with me. What the hell is wrong with the people down here? Who is going to trial here from the gate?

THE COURT You can take him back into the lockup. The Court will appoint an attorney to talk to him.

WITNESS (addressing the defendant) Are you going to trial, brother?

DEFENDANT Yes.

94

WITNESS What's you name?
DEFENDANT (omitted)
WITNESS (still addressing the defendant) What the hell is wrong with these people right here? Big Ike says hello.

9

LEADING QUESTIONS

"The penalty for laughing in a courtroom is six months; if it were not for this penalty the jury would never hear the evidence."

H. L. MENCKEN

"If you can think about something that is related to something else without thinking about the thing to which it is related, then you have the legal mind."

THOMAS REED POWELL

"All interrogatories must, to some extent, make a suggestion to a witness. It would be perfectly nugatory to ask a witness, if he knew anything about something."

LORD LANGDALE

COUNSEL	Did you see any feces on the ground?
WITNESS	I didn't see any—I didn't see any fishes.
COUNSEL	Not fishes, feces.
WITNESS	Little frogs. No I didn't see any.
COUNSEL	When you don't pass water, when you do number two.
WITNESS	What do you mean?
COUNSEL	In other words, did he pass food through his body?
WITNESS	I don't understand.
COUNSEL	Okay. Pardon me ladies and gentlemen. Did he take a shit? Did you see any of that?
WITNESS	I didn't see that, no.
COUNSEL	Did you smell it?
WITNESS	Why should I go and smell his shit?

. . . .

THE COURT	I thought the six-foot fence was to the south?
WITNESS	Well the West Side is kind of confusing. Normally a person would say that north and south runs east and west if you were north of the tracks. And some persons say they would be east and west if you were south of the tracks. So I use north and south. And that's—the report the detective has is opposite. But the way the report has—the way the detective has it in the report, he would have been rolled south, which would have been east, if you can understand what I'm saying.

. . . .

COUNSEL	All right. Was there some event, Valerie, that occurred which kind of finally made you determine that you had to separate from your husband?
WITNESS	Yes.
COUNSEL	Did he try to do something to you?
WITNESS	Yes.
COUNSEL	What did he do?
WITNESS	Well, uh, he tried to kill me.
COUNSEL	All right. And then you felt that that was the last straw; is that correct?
WITNESS	Right.

. . . .

COUNSEL	Is Jerry a man or woman?
WITNESS	A man.
COUNSEL	Do you know where he lives?
WITNESS	No, I do not.
COUNSEL	Do you know his telephone number?
WITNESS	No, I do not. I think Judy do.
COUNSEL	Can you describe him for us?
WITNESS	No, I—I don't know what he looks like. Black.
COUNSEL	He is black?
WITNESS	He is about 6 feet; short afro; has a mustache. I believe him and Judy has a relationship.
COUNSEL	What kind of relationship?
WITNESS	I think they fuck every now and then.

. . . .

WITNESS He was saying he hated Anna and she was a dirty so and so and all this cussing and crap. I started telling him, you know, look, I don't like the cussing and all the stuff.

COUNSEL Does that irritate you, him swearing?

WITNESS Yes, it does.

COUNSEL What'd he do next?

WITNESS With both hands, drug me over to the bed, threw me around and kept choking the shit out of me.

. . . .

COUNSEL Now, in the past you have received numerous threats from the defendant, haven't you?

WITNESS Yes.

COUNSEL And those threats were against—he was threatening your life?

WITNESS Not my life. No, he just threatened to throw battery acid in my face.

. . . .

THE COURT I got the *Quadrafini,* but then he said somebody played in it, and I didn't get that.

PROSECUTOR The Who.

THE COURT The what?

WITNESS Musicians.

PROSECUTOR	The Who.
WITNESS	The Who.
THE COURT	Who?
WITNESS	The Who. That's the name of the band.
THE COURT	So that's the name of the group, The Who?
WITNESS	Yes, The Who.
THE COURT	Not The What? The Who?
WITNESS	No, The Who.
THE COURT	You got it, everybody? The *Quadrafini* is a movie with The Who.
WITNESS	Punk rockers.
THE COURT	All right.

· · · · · · · · · · · · · · ·

THE COURT Would you lift it so I can describe it for the record?

The sergeant is pointing to an area, oh, I would say about two or three inches above his left wrist.

He is holding his left arm extended outward so the left side of his arm and hand are facing me, and it would be just at the spot where the front of the arm becomes the right side and back of the arm.

Is that clear enough for everybody?

· · · · · · · · · · · · · · ·

COUNSEL I'd be glad to make an offer of proof with regard to that question about the tattoo on her breast, but I think it should be made.

THE COURT   The witness, by the way, for the record, just asked me if I'd like to see it; and I said, "No."

WITNESS   I mean, because it's not on my breast. It's right on my chest.

COUNSEL   May the record reflect that she just showed it to everybody in the court?

THE COURT   There it is.

WITNESS   Right there.

THE COURT   Some people call that a breast.

. . . .

D.A.   Have you come into court and lied against Jessie?

WITNESS   No.

D.A.   Have you come to court and lied for Philip?

WITNESS   No.

D.A.   Has anyone told you what to say here in court?

WITNESS   No.

D.A.   Did any police officers tell you what to say here in court?

WITNESS   No.

D.A.   Did Detective C. tell you what to say here in court?

WITNESS   No.

D.A.   What did I tell you to say here in court?

WITNESS   (pause) Stick with the story.

. . . .

COUNSEL Were you leaning up against the shut door
or open door?

WITNESS A shut door. How can you lean against an
open door? There's a hole there. You'd fall
through the hole.

. . . .

COUNSEL Do you think that based upon these
observations that you stated that you had,
and conversations with neighbors, have you
been able to form an opinion as to
whether she is a chaste or unchaste
person?

WITNESS Yes.

COUNSEL And what is your opinion?

WITNESS She is chased and she doesn't chase.
When you go out and flag a guy down—I
mean, you can't help it.

THE COURT Rephrase the question. Apparently the
witness doesn't understand.

COUNSEL Do you know—perhaps I'm not speaking
clearly. Do you know the meaning of the
word "chaste"?

WITNESS No, I'm not sure what you mean.

COUNSEL All right. The word "morality,"
moral-morality versus immorality?

WITNESS I don't believe she has any morals.

. . . .

"Objection, Your Honor. Counsel is leading the witness."

DEFENSE COUNSEL	At any time did you hear any shots being fired?
WITNESS	Yes.
DEFENSE COUNSEL	How many did you hear?
WITNESS	Two at first.
DEFENSE COUNSEL	Okay. And could you tell us how fast those two shots were fired?
WITNESS	Like estimate you mean?
DEFENSE COUNSEL	Yes.
WITNESS	Like bang, bang.
DEFENSE COUNSEL	Okay. Now you recall testifying at the preliminary hearing, correct?
WITNESS	Correct.
DEFENSE COUNSEL	Okay. And at that time do you remember saying that the shots went, as opposed to bang, bang, the shots went bang bang?
WITNESS	What do you mean bang bang?
DEFENSE COUNSEL	Well there is a difference, right, between bang, bang and bang bang?
WITNESS	I said, well I said bang, boom boom is what I said, right?
DEFENSE COUNSEL	Okay. Is that correct, boom boom?
WITNESS	Yes.
DEFENSE COUNSEL	Okay. And is that the way now that you recall the shots being fired, boom boom?
WITNESS	Boom boom. Well, really, the way it is like cap-gun like I said, like more of like a pop. I was saying like boom boom as an example.
DEFENSE COUNSEL	Now can you describe, using whatever words you want, pop, boom, bang,

106

whatever, how fast you heard those shots go off?

WITNESS Boom, boom.

. . . .

PLAINTIFF'S COUNSEL What doctor treated you for the injuries you sustained while at work?

WITNESS Dr. J.

PLAINTIFF'S COUNSEL And what kind of physician is Dr. J.?

WITNESS Well, I'm not sure, but I remember that you said he was a good plaintiff's doctor!

. . . .

COUNSEL Could you briefly describe the type of construction equipment used in your business?

WITNESS Four tractors.

COUNSEL What kind of tractors are they?

WITNESS Fords.

COUNSEL Did you say "four?"

WITNESS Ford. Ford. Like the Ford. It is a Ford tractor.

COUNSEL You didn't say "four," you just said "Ford?"

WITNESS Yes, Ford. That is what you asked me, what kind of tractors.

COUNSEL Are there four Ford tractors? Is that what it is?

WITNESS No, no. You asked me what kind of a tractor it was and I said Ford tractors.

COUNSEL	How many tractors are there?
WITNESS	Four.

. . . .

DEFENSE COUNSEL	The truth of the matter is that you are not an unbiased, objective witness, isn't it? You, too were shot in the fracas?
WITNESS	No, sir. I was shot midway between the fracas and the naval.

. . . .

The defendant herein, having been first duly sworn, was examined and testified as follows:

THE COURT	Mr. Guzman, can you read and write and understand the English language?
DEFENDANT	Si.

10

CROSS EXAMINATION

"More cross-examinations are suicidal than homicidal."
EMORY R. BUCKNER

"Whosoever diggeth a pit shall fall therein: and he that rolleth a stone, it will return upon him."
PROVERBS, 26:27

WITNESS   You know what, I'm tired of this game. I got nothing to say.

D.A.   Did you become familiar, have you become familiar with the convict code?

WITNESS   I'm familiar with a lot of things.

D.A.   And you are familiar with the convict code, right?

WITNESS   I let you assume all that. Because that's all you're doing, your just blowing it out of your ass.

D.A.   Now, under the convict code is it allowed for one convict to testify for the prosecution against another convict?

WITNESS   You know how I will answer that? Two easy ways [holds up middle two fingers] subtract one [vulgar gesture].

D.A.   And as you sit there today, you have a very strong dislike for me, correct?

WITNESS   For you, your mother, your dog, your grandfather, everybody else about you.

D.A.   And the reason that you very strongly dislike me is because of the fact that you feel I'm placing your life in danger by calling you as a witness, right?

WITNESS   You want to know? Currently, I'm housed in Folsom Prison and by you calling me down here, you fuck me out of my handball games. I had a hundred dollars money game going. You going to compensate me for that?

D.A.   That's the only reason why you dislike me as the prosecutor, right?

WITNESS   I'm a capitalist at heart.

. . . .

DEFENSE COUNSEL Answer the question. When did they have a knife at your throat?

WITNESS That was a figure of speech.

DEFENSE COUNSEL So they had a figure of speech at your throat?

. . . .

PROSECUTOR You remember Good Friday, don't you? Do you remember what the previous Sunday, May 14th was? What date it was?

WITNESS That Sunday before the 17th of May?

PROSECUTOR Uh-huh.

WITNESS I believe it was Mother's Day.

PROSECUTOR Were you thinking of your mother when you committed that homicide?

DEFENSE COUNSEL Your Honor, I would object to that as argumentative.

PROSECUTOR Or your mother-in-law?

THE COURT Sustained.

PROSECUTOR Do you remember what May 20th, 1978, it was the following Saturday?

WITNESS May 20th I was in jail.

PROSECUTOR You don't know what day it was? That was Armed Forces Day, wasn't it?

THE COURT I wonder whether that is a material test of his recollection. I have flown in combat and I don't know when Armed Forces Day is, but maybe some people do. All right.

PROSECUTOR But you remember what day Good Friday was? You had to come in and tell us that, what day Good Friday was?

WITNESS Yes. I remember what day Good Friday was on.

PROSECUTOR You know who gets condemned more than even liars and killers in the Scripture? Well, let me ask you, do you know what a hypocrite is?

DEFENSE COUNSEL Once again, I would object to that.

THE COURT Sustained, argumentative.

. . . .

PROSECUTOR You pretty much hate the defendant though, don't you?

WITNESS No, not really. I just think he is a crazy kid. That's all.

PROSECUTOR Didn't you describe him before as a punk, liar, thief, cheat and murderer and the lowest form of life that you know?

WITNESS Yeah. That pretty well sums him up. But he is a crazy kid on top of that.

. . . .

COUNSEL Were you ever in the military service?

WITNESS I was.

COUNSEL And when were you in the military service?

WITNESS World War II.

COUNSEL And what years were they?

WITNESS	September 1939 until April 1945.
COUNSEL	And during that period of time was it not a fact that there was segregation in the Armed Forces?
D.A.	Your Honor, I'd object as irrelevant.
COUNSEL	Bias.
THE COURT	Segregation? On what grounds?
COUNSEL	Racial grounds.
WITNESS	Not to my knowledge.
COUNSEL	You are not aware that the Armed Forces —that Truman in 1944 ordered the desegregation of Armed Forces?
D.A.	I object as irrelevant.
THE COURT	The objection is sustained.
COUNSEL	I think the court can take judicial notice the Armed Forces were segregated by race until Truman ordered them desegregated as President of the United States.
WITNESS	I was in the Canadian Army.

. . . .

COUNSEL	Do you know whether they were 45 records or those big ones?
WITNESS	Yes, 45.
COUNSEL	They were little 45 records?
WITNESS	Yes.
COUNSEL	Do you remember what the song was, Mabel?
WITNESS	"Things I Used To Do I Won't Do No More."
COUNSEL	"Things I Used To Do I Won't Do No More?"

"All right, you two! Break it up!"

WITNESS	That's that record. You ask George [the defendant] there. I play that all time. Can I talk to him? Is that right, George? That's what I play, ain't it?
THE COURT	Wait a minute. You can't talk to the defendant.
WITNESS	Well, I asked him could I.
THE COURT	You'll have to ask me. I run this here business.
WITNESS	Oh, well, I'm sorry. I didn't think you knowed the record; you wasn't up there.
THE COURT	The only record I know is, "What Lilbert [the deceased] used to know, Lilbert don't know no more."
WITNESS	Yeah, he's played his last one.

. . . .

D.A.	Mr. C., you testified on your direct examination that quote it takes a lots to make me angry. Close quote. Is that true?
WITNESS	Yes, because I don't like to get angry. I feel I can resolve problems without getting angry. The only time I may be offensive is if someone attack me.
D.A.	You figure you're a basically peaceful person?
WITNESS	I tries to be.
D.A.	Your wife is named Willetta, is that correct?
WITNESS	Yes.

D.A.   On December the 19th, 1981, did you hit
         Willetta in the face with a two-by-four?
WITNESS It was not a two-by-four. It was a
         one-by-three.

11

EXPERT WITNESSES

"*I am firmly of the belief that jurors are quite capable of seeing through flaky testimony and pseudo-scientific clap-trap. I quite agree that we should not waste our valuable court time watching witch doctors, voo-doo practitioners, or brujas go through the entrails of dead chickens in a fruitless search for the truth.*"

JUSTICE ROBERT A. GARDNER

"*Expert opinion is only an ordinary guess in evening clothes.*"

JUSTICE CURTIS BOK

"*There are three kinds of witnesses: liars, damned liars, and experts.*"

ANONYMOUS

COUNSEL	And you are involved I take it in both aspects of pathology here in your practice?
WITNESS	Yes. I am certified in both.
COUNSEL	Directing your attention to the 6th of November 1976, in the evening hours, do you recall being up at Rose Chapel in Paradise?
WITNESS	Yes.
COUNSEL	Do you recall examining a person by the name of Rodney Edgington at the funeral chapel?
WITNESS	Yes.
COUNSEL	Do you recall approximately the time that you examined the body of Mr. Edgington at the Rose Chapel?
WITNESS	It was in the evening. The autopsy started at about 8:30 P.M.
COUNSEL	And Mr. Edginton was dead at that time, is that correct?
WITNESS	No, you dumb asshole. He was sitting on the table wondering why I was doing an autopsy.

. . . .

DEFENSE COUNSEL	Are there some types of rules or a code of ethics among prostitutes and their employer?
D.A.	Objection. It calls for an expert opinion. It's also vague as to time and place.
THE COURT	Foundation, counsel. I don't believe there is any foundation for this.

121

D.A.   May I take the witness on *voir dire?*

THE COURT   Yes.

D.A.   Mr. P, pimps don't have organizations like other professions have, do they?

WITNESS   They are organized.

D.A.   Are there conventions where pimps get together and discuss mutual problems and things of that nature?

WITNESS   They have what you would call pimp conventions.

D.A.   Mr. P., do you consider yourself to be a student of pimpology or the study of pimping?

WITNESS   Well, I have hung around a lot of them.

D.A.   Any particular reason why?

WITNESS   Because I wanted to know about it. I wanted to know the different backgrounds, the ways that they ran their system and the motions, the steps, because I wanted to make mine different.

. . . .

D.A.   What is the meaning of sperm being present?

WITNESS   It indicates intercourse.

D.A.   Male sperm?

WITNESS   That is the only kind I know.

. . . .

COUNSEL   Doctor, would you be surprised if you saw the defendant talking to himself?

WITNESS   Not in the least.

COUNSEL   Why is that?

WITNESS   He doesn't have any friends.

. . . .

PROSECUTOR   Would you briefly describe your background with respect to bullets and ammunition?

DEFENSE COUNSEL   I am going to object to this, Your Honor, unless the district attorney can make an offer of proof that this man is an expert, and I don't want to hear that he has been shooting bullets since he was ten.

THE COURT   It will be overruled.

WITNESS   I have been interested in shooting basically since I was ten years old, both cartridge-type ammunition and also black power. I do my own reloading for my guns. I have a reloading press at home and powder and all that stuff.

PROSECUTOR   What is your background with respect to .22 ammunition?

WITNESS   I have purchased a lot of it.

. . . .

COUNSEL   The respiratory arrest means no breathing, doesn't it?

WITNESS   That's right.

COUNSEL   And in every case where there is a death, isn't there no breathing?

. . . .

DEFENSE ATTORNEY	How would you expect somebody to react being stabbed six times in this fashion?
WITNESS	At one point as he is being stabbed he is going to hurt.
DEFENSE ATTORNEY	And would that be debilitating in any way, limit somebody's ability to move around or to function in any way?
WITNESS	It might slow him down a little.

. . . .

COUNSEL	OK. Now, let's translate that, doctor. Reddish discoloration is a more recent sort of injury; is that correct?
WITNESS	More fresh.
COUNSEL	Fresh?
WITNESS	More fresh.
COUNSEL	More fresh.
WITNESS	Not fresh fresh, but more fresh than recent.

. . . .

COUNSEL	Now, you also testified that you tried to run a test that the matter was cocaine, is that right?
POLICE OFFICER	I tried to run a water test on it.
COUNSEL	What did the test consist of?
POLICE OFFICER	The substance looked something like soap powder, so we ran water in the portable

bar that was in the room and the sergeant tried to see what would happen to the cocaine as the water hit it.

COUNSEL What was supposed to have happened?

POLICE OFFICER If it was cocaine it would have immediately have dissolved.

COUNSEL What would have happened if that was soap?

POLICE OFFICER It would have dissolved.

. . . .

COUNSEL Are you qualified to give a urine sample?

WITNESS Yes, I have been since early childhood.

. . . .

DEFENSE COUNSEL So if I hit the prosecutor at this very moment and he fell over the back of this railing, hit his head and a subdural hematoma immediately began to form, the blood that was leaking into the space would have essentially the same components as the blood leaking into his teeny little brain?

. . . .

THE COURT In this case the request is made for the appointment of the psychologist for the performance of an IQ test. The court does not see the need for an IQ test since it

appears to me that he is dumber than a
fencepost.

COUNSEL   Has the court stated it in numerical
terms?

THE COURT   His IQ is less than zero.

. . . .

COUNSEL   What device do you have in your
laboratory to test alcohol content?

WITNESS   I have a dual column gas chromatograph,
Hewlett-Packard 5710A with flame
analyzation detectors.

THE COURT   Can you get that with mag wheels?

WITNESS   Only on the floor models.

. . . .

COUNSEL   Could you describe your duties as a
forensic analyst?

WITNESS   I analyze narcotics; I analyze blood, breath
and urine samples for alcohol, I analyze
blood and urine samples for drugs. I
analyze all types of physical evidence for
blood, and I do sex fiend cases, assault
cases, homicide cases, anything like that.

. . . .

COUNSEL   Let me rephrase it. It was kind of poorly
phrased.

THE COURT   Most of your questions are, but that's
okay. Want to start over?

"May I ask you to call for quiet, Your Honor? My witness is about to share his expertise."

COUNSEL   If you had estimated the fetal weight as of August 15, 1978, do you have any opinion as to what your estimate would have been?

WITNESS   I think that's impossible. I don't any—I—I don't think I could answer it, because I don't think I know.

You're asking me to guess what I would have guessed if I had tried to guess, and I didn't try to guess; so I don't know what I would have tried to guess or what I would have guessed.

. . . .

Argument heading in an appellant's opening brief:

THE TRIAL COURT ERRED IN ORDERING A MEDICAL EXAMINATION OF APPELLANT'S PENIS IN HIS ABSENCE.

COUNSEL   Now, in your report under "Foundation" you indicated there is a minimum of cracking and no signs of settling.

WITNESS   Yes.

COUNSEL   When you say there is a minimum of cracking, I take it that you did find some cracking.

WITNESS   No. Because if I said there was no

cracking, I would be in court just like this answering some stupid lawyers' questions. So I put minimum in there to cover myself, because somebody is going to find a crack somewhere.

THE COURT I could say I would like to shake your hand, but I won't.

COUNSEL Move to strike—

THE COURT No. We are not going to strike it.

COUNSEL Move to strike the word "stupid," Your Honor.

THE COURT The most appropriate word you want stricken? It is worth the whole trial.

. . . .

The following ad was placed in the Los Angeles *Daily Journal* on April 8, 1980:

Alienist Wanted
"Alphabet Bomber," Chief Military Officer of "Aliens of America," acting in propria persona, is seeking the assistance of an alienist, capable of advanced intellectual gymnastics, (yet free of the side effects of intellectual hallucinogens and ideological brain damage), and interested in defining a scientific formula of the relationship of intellectual and mental competence within the meaning of 1368 PC and as applied to a condition where a defendant in a mass murder trial

believes to be The Messiah, and has set up his own arrest due to his "delusion" that he must prove in the court of law of the "City of Angels" that he is The Messiah, and thus establish the legality of his world rulership.

This project presupposes one's ability to temporarily case away all socio-religious illusions and traditions and base one's thinking entirely on cold facts in total absence of emotion, and this project shall be illuminated by the presumption of innocence; by the classic example of the difference between sane and insane; (2,000 years ago a man who believed that earth is round was insane and today a man who believes that earth is flat is insane); by the scientific truths that there is an exception to every rule; and by the historical truths that the might defines the right.

This project is neither an opportunity for a $50 an hour license owning babelist, nor a $100 an hour cloud-riding conclusionist, but an opportunity for a young, unbrainwashed, tradition uninhibited, ideology immune, methodic scientist.

12

CREATIVE DEFENSES

"Justice is not to be taken by storm. She is to be wooed by slow advances."

JUSTICE BENJAMIN N. CARDOZO

"I will look, Your Honor, and endeavor to find a precedent, if you require it; though it would seem to be a pity that the Court should lose the honor of being the first to establish so just a rule."

RUFUS CHOATE

DEFENDANT   What records I had, I had in my garage. I got a Labrador dog that floats over a seven-foot fence like an airplane. He is on probation, and if he bites one more person we are going to put him to sleep. For the last two years, he's been kept in my garage. He ate up a couch, so I mean the records where I have them stacked on this table, he completely ate them all, and some we are able to save, and we are in the process, which I told my attorney, and I have been spending a lot of time in trying to get these records straight.

COUNSEL   What records are those? This is the first we have heard about this. We have asked you questions about records. This is the first time we hear the dog defense.

. . . .

OFFER OF PROOF   It was defendant's position that due to his limited education, background and experience, and his alleged cultural deficiencies, he lacked the wherewithal to perpetrate the evasion of his federal income tax. To this end, defendant intended to call Dr. Bruce to testify as to his findings with respect to defendant's intellectual capacity based upon certain tests and examinations conducted by him on the defendant. His defense was simply that he was too stupid willfully to violate the Internal Revenue Code and that the expert would testify as to the defendant's stupidity.

THE COURT In this matter, the Court is, of course, aware of the explanation given by the defendant for his reason for having this particular weapon in his possession at the time the search was made of his home. And, as I recall, he stated that he had possession of the weapon in order to change the holster for the weapon from a right-handed to left-handed holster, which he proposed to do by reversing it or turning the holster inside out. An examination of the holster would indicate that that proposal was ridiculous and I think the jury found the explanation equally ridiculous and convicted him of the charge.

COUNSEL Your Honor, you heard the matter without a jury.

THE COURT I did?

COUNSEL Yes.

THE COURT Then I found it ridiculous.

. . . .

DEFENSE COUNSEL I am prepared to go to trial on this case. Now, my investigator fully investigated this case. I have talked to the defendant several times; he advises me that before we go to trial certain things must be done.

Number one, he wants to have a
professional makeup man get him up in
several different disguises.

. . . .

THE COURT	How do you plead at this time, guilty or not guilty of the charges?
DEFENDANT	Not guilty by reason of total love.
COUNSEL	Your Honor, I would indicate first that when I spoke with him today he had indicated that he wished to proceed pro per representing himself.
DEFENDANT	That is right, Your Honor.
THE COURT	Why is that?
DEFENDANT	Because I am the only one that can try this case properly, and I am very well talented. I have fifteen years studying canon law.
THE COURT	Which kind of law?
DEFENDANT	Canon law that all laws are based on. The laws of God apply to all cases. Canon law is the law of Moses, is that not right? And the Ten Commandments are the law of Moses. All laws are based on the Ten Commandments; so they have to derive and come from them, right?
THE COURT	No, no, no. I am not going to allow you to represent yourself at this point.
DEFENDANT	I have already passed the psychiatric examinations, three of them. Dr. Morgan has given me a total far out. Dr. Morgan

135

is a Christian. He believes like I do.

THE COURT   He's given you a total far out, is that what you said?

DEFENDANT   As a matter of fact, Your Honor, he said if Jesus Christ was in jail He'd be sitting with me in my same cell. Do I need any more?

. . . .

COUNSEL   Yes. Has Mollie Frickle [the deceased] ever threatened you in any manner?

WITNESS   Yes.

COUNSEL   On more than one occasion?

WITNESS   Yes.

COUNSEL   Would you describe any injuries that you have suffered at her hands.

WITNESS   On numerous occasions she's taken out a knife and threw it at me. But, the only injury I can truthfully say I ever suffered is when she grabbed me by the ear, you know, and with a knife, just—what can I say? Tore my ear. I guess that's the only thing, she tore my ear. She scratched it like this and tore my ear.

COUNSEL   Did your ear bleed as a result of that?

WITNESS   Only for four weeks.

COUNSEL   Did she ever make any verbal threats to you as to what she would do to you?

WITNESS   Yes.

COUNSEL   What did she say in that regard?

WITNESS   She said she was going to cut my balls off.

136

"In extenuation, Your Honor, may I point out that my
client cannot read English?"

. . . [S]he threatened me, the time she threatened Mike, the time she threatened Herman, my son, my cousin, her brother. She was a vile old lady. On numerous occasions, more than once and less than a thousand, but on numerous occasions she told Mike that his girl friend was a triple cunted whore. I am not sure what that means. I assume that it means that—

COUNSEL   Sir, do you recall anything that—anything in particular that Mollie Frickle said she would do to the defendant?

WITNESS   Yes.

COUNSEL   Can you tell us what that was?

WITNESS   I—on one occasion she said she was going to cut his balls off, and this is the way Mollie Frickle talked, and put them in a washing machine and just flush them like down to Long Beach.

COUNSEL   How old was Mollie Frickle at the time of her death, if you know?

WITNESS   Seventy-seven, seventy-two, I guess.

. . . .

COUNSEL   And what happened after you had been listening to the music for awhile?

WITNESS   We got held up.

COUNSEL   And what happened? Would you give the judge the details of that?

WITNESS   Well, they told us to get up against the wall, throw our money on the floor, and drop our pants.

138

COUNSEL   And what did you do?

WITNESS   Got against the wall, threw my pants down, and threw our money down.

COUNSEL   I mean after you got up against the wall and went through—or followed his directions, what happened?

WITNESS   Cracked up laughing, because one of the other guys—guys in on it dropped his pants, too.

COUNSEL   Excuse me. One of the robbers?

WITNESS   Right.

COUNSEL   He took off his pants, also?

WITNESS   Right.

COUNSEL   And what happened as he did that?

WITNESS   They told him, "Not you stupid." And he picked up the money.

13

CLOSING ARGUMENT

"*Wisdom too often never comes, and so one ought not to reject it merely because it comes late.*"

JUSTICE FELIX FRANKFURTER

"*He can compress the most words into the smallest idea of any man I ever met.*"

ABRAHAM LINCOLN

A criminal defense lawyer is making his closing argument to the jury. His client is accused of murder, but the body of the victim has never been found. He dramatically withdraws his pocket watch and announces to the jury, "Ladies and gentlemen, I have some astounding news. We have found the supposed victim of this murder alive and well, and, in exactly one minute, he will walk through that door into this courtroom."

A hushed silence falls over the courtroom, as everyone waits for the momentous entry. Nothing happens.

The lawyer then says, "The mere fact that you were watching that door, expecting the victim to walk into this courtroom, suggests that you have a reasonable doubt whether a murder was committed." Pleased with the impact of the stunt, he then sits down to await an acquittal.

The jury is instructed, files out and files back in 10 minutes later with a verdict finding the defendant guilty. Following the proceedings, the astounded lawyer chases after the jury foreman to find out what went wrong. "How could you convict?" he asks. "You were all watching the door!"

The foreman explains, "Most of us were watching the door. But one of us was watching the defendant, and he wasn't watching the door."

. . . .

DEFENSE COUNSEL   I think one particular remark my client was offended by that the D.A. made was his exhortation to the jury to convict the defendant in order to celebrate the Bicentennial.

. . . .

PROSECUTOR   Now, my personal opinion as to whether or not he's guilty, that doesn't mean a thing, because I have not testified in this case. But defense counsel gave his opinion, and I'm going to give you mine. The son-of-a-bitch (indicating) is guilty as hell.

D.A.   I told you I thought the defense counsel was throwing out a lot of red herrings in this case. About halfway through this trial I believe that you sensed something smelled funny here. Here's what that smell is coming from (whereupon, the D.A. presented the defense lawyer with a pile of cow manure mounted on a plaque. A motion for mistrial was denied.)

. . . .

Defense Argument To Jury In Prostitution Case

Now, you know, sex is as old as the world, ladies and gentlemen, and it will

be bought and sold whether you
condemn it here or choose to look the
other way. Well, for my client, this is a
serious case. For the government, it is a
serious case. But you know, for anyone
with a little common sense, this case is
an extravagant folly; cops flown in from
Indiana, Minnesota, Missouri, Georgia,
Michigan, FBI from Washington,
handwriting expert, hotel detectives from
Louisiana, a hotel detective who can't
remember which room it was in, and his
report can't help you straighten it out,
motel records from all over, pounds of
paper, movie screens, fancy projectors. A
huge production. For what? Organized
crime? No. Bank robbers? No. Hijackers?
No. For what? For kids selling pussy.

D.A.'S Entire Closing Argument In A Drunk Driving Case

Roses are red
Violets are blue
Point one five
means drunk to you.

The verdict was guilty.

. . . .

D.A.   All you have to decide is whether based on
the evidence that you've heard you're

satisfied beyond a reasonable doubt that
that's the man.

I read a story in *Reader's Digest* the
other day. Seems there were two attorneys.
And one attorney was married, and he had
a suspicion that when he would go out of
town to interview clients or make court
appearances in other cities, that his wife
was carrying on with a younger man.

So he got this friend of his, who was
available in the evening, and he said to his
friend, "Would you mind for the next
three days, while I'm gone, to sort of keep
an eye out on my wife and on our house
and see whether she has any visitors, and
let me know about it when I come back?"

So this second lawyer did that. And he
sort of hid in the weeds across the street
from the first lawyer's house. And, sure
enough, the following night, a car pulled
up, and a young man got out and went in
the house. And the lawyer sat there and
he watched all of this going on. And he
was taking notes on his legal pad, that all
lawyers carry with them at all times.

At the end of the evening when his
report was finished, he got on the phone
and he called the other attorney, the
attorney who lived in this house. And he
told the attorney, "I saw this car drive up;
I saw this young man get out; I saw him
go to the door, knock on it; a couple of

"But perhaps I digress."

minutes later, the door opened, and your wife opened the door and let him in."

And the attorney said, "Well, what happened then?" And the other guy said, "Well then I saw them go in the living room and they sat down; they talked for a little while, and then your wife got up, and she went into the kitchen. And she opened the refrigerator, pulled out a half gallon of wine, she poured a couple of glasses of wine, brought them into the living room and the two of them sat there and they drank the wine."

And the husband said, "What happened then?"

And the other lawyer said, "And then when they finished the wine, they got up, and she took his hand and then I saw them walk out of the living room and then they disappeared from my view."

And then the lawyer said, "Well, what happened then?" And the other lawyer said, "Well, then I saw the light come on upstairs, then I saw the two of them come into the bedroom, and I saw them embrace and kiss."

And the husband said, "Well, what happened then?" And the other lawyer said, "Well, your wife went over and turned out the light switch and I couldn't see anything that happened after that."

And the husband said, "Damn, that reasonable doubt."

I don't think I really have to expand on that story, ladies and gentlemen. There's no reasonable doubt in this case. There's a possible doubt. But there's no reasonable doubt.

14

JURY INSTRUCTIONS
AND DELIBERATIONS

"The naive assumption that prejudicial effects can be overcome by instructions to the jury . . . all practicing lawyers know to be unmitigated fiction."

JUSTICE ROBERT H. JACKSON

"Grand conglomerations of garbled verbiage and verbal garbage."
CHANNING POLLACK

JUROR	Your Honor, is it proper to ask the interpreter a question? I'm uncertain about the word la vado. You say that is a bar.
THE COURT	The court cannot permit jurors to ask questions directly. If you want to phrase your question to me—
JUROR	I understood it to be a restroom. I could better believe they would meet in a restroom rather than a public bar if he is undercover.
THE COURT	These are matters for you to consider. If you have any misunderstanding of what the witness testified to, tell the court now what you didn't understand and we'll place the—
JUROR	I understand the word la vado—I thought it meant restroom. She translates it as bar.
INTERPRETER	In the first place, the jurors are not to listen to the Spanish but to the English. I am a certified court interpreter.
JUROR	You're an idiot.

. . . .

Defendant's proposed instruction no. 7 assumption of risk:

> You are hereby instructed that when a person makes a decision to become a drug dealer he assumes the risk of: (1) being shot; (2) being killed; (3) being robbed; and (4) all of the above. 1 Rex 12 (1392).

Defendant's Proposed Instruction
No. 8:

> You are hereby instructed that any-
> body who kills four drug dealers can't be
> all bad.

After the jury had been deliberating for
approximately six hours they came back into
the courtroom and asked for instructions on
premeditation, deliberation and specific intent.

THE COURT   I understand that you are confused by my
instructions on premeditation, deliteration
and Pacific intent. Those will now be read
back to you.

JURY FOREMAN   Your Honor, we would really just like to
take the written instructions back into the
jury room.

THE COURT   Okay, does counsel have any objections?

COUNSEL   No, Your Honor, but we would also like
them to have instructions on
preverification, deterioration and Atlantic
intent.

JURORS   [Laugh.]

D.A.   I think we should also throw in the Indian
Ocean Instruction.

THE COURT   Where have you guys been hiding out
during these deliberations?

COUNSEL   With you, Your Honor.

. . . .

The defendant challenged his conviction on grounds the jury that tried him conducted an unconstitutional experiment to check key evidence in his case.

The woman he was convicted of raping had testified she bit her assailant on the arm during the attack, but could not identify the defendant.

The prosecution relied on police photographs of a bruise on one of the defendant's arms when he was arrested and on a doctor's testimony that the bruise was caused by human teeth.

The defendant said he was bruised when he scraped his arm on a chain-link fence the night of the rape.

The jury, in trying to make up its mind, conducted an experiment in which a woman juror bit the foreman's arm.

The jurors then made periodic checks on the resulting bruise and compared it with the photos of the defendant's arm.

. . . .

After three to four hours of deliberation the jury indicated they were hung. The judge asked them if further proceedings could result in a verdict. The foreman replied that they had taken a vote on whether or not they were hung and that vote was 6 to 6.

. . . .

The judge received the following note from the jury as they were deliberating a case:

"The jury stands at 10 to 2. One juror is obsessed with proof of intent. One juror sought guidance of prayer and was answered by God in her decision. Please instruct."

. . . .

The eight-man, four-woman jury had been deliberating for 20 hours when, at 5:30 P.M., it found itself still stuck at 9 to 3 in favor of conviction.

Within a few minutes, the judge received a note from the foreman: "Juror number 10 has locked herself in the girl's restroom. She has not responded to our notes. What shall we do?"

The juror refused to respond to other jurors when they talked to her from the other side of the restroom door. She remained holed up there for more than 15 minutes.

After receiving the foreman's note, the judge asked the other jurors to come back into the courtroom. Meanwhile, the bailiff successfully coaxed juror number 10 out of the restroom.

The judge declared a mistrial.

"We find the defense incompetent, the prosecution arrogant, the food inedible, the accommodations insufferable, and the defendant guilty as Hell."

. . . .

DEFENSE COUNSEL   At this time I would request, since a
motion is going to be held in this
courtroom, a motion to suppress
identification from the victim of a
particular lineup, that the jury be excused
from the jury room. I believe they can
hear the testimony which will be presented
in the courtroom.

THE COURT   Let the record show that we are in a five
million dollar courthouse, that this is the
courtroom where the case has been
assigned, that it's a brand new jury room,
well insulated; that the jury is in the jury
room and it is the opinion of the court
that they can't hear anything that is going
on because the jury is presently conversing
and we can't hear them.

DEFENSE COUNSEL   How do we know they are conversing?

THE COURT   Can't you hear them?

. . . .

THE COURT   Have you arrived at a verdict?

FOREMAN   Yes, we have.

THE COURT   Please give the verdicts to the bailiff.
Please read them.

CLERK   "We the jury impaneled to try the
above-entitled cause find the defendant
guilty."

JUROR   Wait a minute!

CLERK   I am sorry, Your Honor. That's wrong.
        This isn't signed.
THE COURT   This isn't signed? What did you read it
        for? Start again.
            Looks like you won't have your job very
        long after this, I can assure you.
CLERK   "We the jury impaneled to try the
        above-entitled cause find the defendant
        not guilty."

. . . .

    The judge was finishing his oral charge
to a jury. Being a judge who keeps up with
the times, he pointed out in the verdict
form where the "foreperson" should sign
the verdict.
    When the verdict was delivered later to
the courtroom deputy, four persons had
signed their names on the form.
    He now uses the old-fashioned word
"foreman."

159

15

SENTENCING

"My object all sublime,
I shall achieve in time,
To let the punishment fit the crime,
The punishment fit the crime."
　　　THE MIKADO
　　　(ARTHUR S. GILBERT)

THE COURT	I suppose the money found on the defendant at the time of his arrest came from this liquor store robbery.
DEFENDANT	No, that was bank robbery money.
THE COURT	Has anyone led you to believe the governor will pardon you if you plead guilty?
DEFENDANT	Well, I haven't been home, Judge, but he might have called my mother.

· · · · · · · · · · · · · · · ·

The judge found himself locked outside his chambers along with the defendant and his defense attorney.

The defendant was about to be sentenced for a burglary conviction.

The judge called for a courthouse worker.

He tried keys, credit cards and a small drill, but failed to open the door.

"If you don't mind, Judge," said the defense lawyer, "I think my client can do this. He has a certain amount of expertise in this."

The judge approved. In three seconds his door was open. The judge thanked the defendant profusely.

"It was nothing at all, Judge, just professional courtesy," the defendant mumbled.

Minutes later, the judge sentenced him

163

to the maximum sentence—10 years in the state prison.

"If I need him again, I know where he will be," he said.

. . . .

An auto theft suspect who successfully applied for a bail reduction was returned to his cell, where he began yelling, cursing and making threats. His jailers hauled him back into court.

THE COURT   What's the problem?

DEFENDANT   [Profanities and insults.] If you ever want to tell me anything, mail it to me.

THE COURT   I won't have to mail you this—I'm finding you in contempt of court and sending you to county jail for one year.

DEFENDANT   Why not make it five years?

THE COURT   All right, you've got it.

DEFENDANT   Why not make it ten years?

THE COURT   You've got it—ten years in county jail.

DEFENDANT   Why not raise my bail to $50,000?

THE COURT   Bail will be set at $100,000.

. . . .

THE COURT   It is the judgment of this court that you be sentenced to the state prison at Deer Lodge for a term of ten years, the maximum penalty.

D.A.   Will that be dangerous or nondangerous offender, Your Honor?

THE COURT Well, considering the flagrant nature of his offense, the court finds that he's a dangerous offender.

DEFENDANT How in the hell can you find me a dangerous offender? There's nothing in there showing any violent crime. What's wrong with everybody anyway? You take that son-of-a-bitch and—

THE COURT That will be it; you're remanded to the custody of the sheriff.

DEFENDANT You son-of-a-bitch. You bald-headed son-of-a-bitch, when I get out of there, I'll blow your fucking head away. You no-good bald-headed son-of-a-bitch.

THE COURT Get that down in the record, he's threatened to blow the judge's head off.

DEFENDANT Stick it in your mouth you bald-headed bastard. You fucking son-of-a-bitch. You no-good bald-headed son-of-a-bitch.

THE COURT If I could, I'd give you another ten years.

. . . .

. . . on a date to be hereafter fixed by order of this Court, within the State Prison, at which time and place you shall then and there put to death the said [defendant] in the manner prescribed by law. [But] . . . the Court finds you are entitled to credit for 549 days for time served and 182 days good time and work time, for a total of 731 days . . .

165

. . . .

THE COURT	All right. Any other questions?
DEFENDANT	How can you sentence an innocent man to prison?
THE COURT	It is part of my job.

. . . .

THE COURT	Is there anything else you would like to say before I pass sentence?
DEFENDANT	Yes, Kirk to Enterprise—Beam me up.

Probation Report Excerpt

The defendant gave the following brief story of his life:

"I am youseley a home tipe of person you no tv music the you will think I all so lick cars going to the drive in is one of my things I hope that all thing come to an end at the drive in."

Education:

The defendant entered school in September 1965. He stated that the last school he attended was at San Diego City College. He stated he successfully completed his GED. The defendant appears to be of average intelligence and literacy.

. . . .

Sentencing

The defendant is an inveterate
womanizer and a golf hustler. In short,
he has no redeeming virtues.

. . . .

The undersigned officer has contacted
the defendant's wife, but she will have
nothing to do with him.

. . . .

Although somewhat large for his age,
Tony appears somewhat smaller than he
actually is.

. . . .

He indicated his marriage was happy,
as he and his wife have always been
sexually combatible.

. . . .

The boy was arrested for petty theft
after the Earl Warren Junior High was
broken in two.

. . . .

Defendant was seen loitering around a
public restroom for the purpose of a lewd
and lascivious act, namely the organ
pavillion in the park.

· · · · · · · · · · · · · · ·

Defendant has been a crook all his life and is still in the restaurant business.

· · · · · · · · · · · · · · ·

He was arrested for disturbing the peach.

· · · · · · · · · · · · · · ·

This boy, a surfer, gets along well with his pier group.

· · · · · · · · · · · · · · ·

The eldest and the youngest children were gone, but the two middle-aged children were still at home.

· · · · · · · · · · · · · · ·

Subject owes no one but the finance company for his car and his mother.

· · · · · · · · · · · · · · ·

Defendant went to county hospital for treatment of cut finger which he cut accidentally while trying to cut wrist in suicide attempt.

· · · · · · · · · · · · · · ·

"25 years! You call that revolving door justice?"

The defendant has made his own bed and now the probation officer feels that he should sleep in it.

. . . .

The man died, but he went to court and beat the case anyway.

. . . .

The defendant is charged with the theft of a roast from a meat market. The defendant acknowledged that before going to the market he pre-heated his oven.

. . . .

This twenty-three-and-a-half-year old defendant appears before the Court today for sentencing following alleged violations of his Superior Court probation grant on the convicted offense of robbery. He wishes this Court to believe that he has not lied to the probation officer and desires to remain on probation to "get a fresh start." If defendant received a nickel for every lie he has told, his net worth would rival the estate of the late Howard Hughes. His daily existence is so thoroughly interlaced with fabrication and deception that it is doubtful that he knows the truth. Whether he acquired the alias of "Watergate" from his unabated burglaries or from his use of Mr. Walter Gate's stolen business cards, remains to be seen. What is seen, as reported by the defendant's own mother and others, is that he has been terrorizing the west side of San Bernardino with his continual stealing.

To this officer, the most difficult problem in preparing this report was in finding the appropriate euphemisms needed to describe the character and behavior of defendant without risking a contempt of court charge. Suffice it to say that he is an abject pathological liar, a thief, and a plague upon the community. So long as he remains on the streets, he will represent a continued threat to the safety and property of innocent members of society. He is a true sociopath, showing no remorse for his actions and no regard whatsoever for the rights of other individuals.

In no way should he be reinstated on supervised probation. He has proven he does not have the capacity to function under supervision. All his psychic energy is used in creating lies for the probation officer, while all his physical energy is spent on stealing. Although the disposition appears too lenient for the crime of robbery, innocent members of the community will at least be spared defendant's foot through their front door for sixteen months.